GETTING TO KNOW THE WORLD'S GREATEST ARTISTS

CAMILLE
PISSARRO

WRITTEN AND ILLUSTRATED BY MIKE VENEZIA

CHILDREN'S PRESS®
A DIVISION OF SCHOLASTIC INC.
NEW YORK TORONTO LONDON AUCKLAND SYDNEY
MEXICO CITY NEW DELHI HONG KONG
DANBURY, CONNECTICUT

For Dave. Thanks for bringing a special touch of color to my books.

Cover: *St. Charles, Eragny, at Sunset,* by Camille Pissarro. 1891, oil on canvas, 80.8 x 64.93 cm.
© Sterling and Francine Clark Art Institute, Williamstown, MA.

Colorist for illustrations: Dave Ludwig

Library of Congress Cataloging-in-Publication Data

Venezia, Mike.
  Camille Pissarro / written and illustrated by Mike Venezia.
    p. cm. — (Getting to know the world's greatest artists)
Summary: Describes the life and work of the nineteenth-century French
painter Camille Pissarro.
  ISBN 0-516-22577-4 (lib. bdg.)   0-516-26977-1 (pbk.)
  1. Pissarro, Camille, 1830-1903—Juvenile literature. 2.
Painters—France—Biography—Juvenile literature. [1. Pissarro, Camille,
1830-1903. 2. Artists. 3. Painting, French.] I. Title. II. Series:
Venezia, Mike. Getting to know the world's greatest artists.
  ND553.P55 V46 2003
  759.4—dc21
                      2002015128

CHILDREN'S PRESS and associated logos are trademarks
and or registered trademarks of Scholastic Library Publishing.
SCHOLASTIC and associated logos are trademarks and or
registered trademarks of Scholastic Inc.

1 2 3 4 5 6 7 8 9 10 R 12 11 10 09 08 07 06 05 04 03

Camille Pissarro was born in 1830 on the Caribbean island of St. Thomas. When he grew up, he moved to Paris, France. There he became an important member of a famous group of artists known as the Impressionists.

Self-Portrait, by Claude Monet. 1917, oil on canvas, 70 x 55 cm. © Art Resource, NY/Réunion des Musées Nationaux, photo by J.G. Berizzi/ Artists Rights Society (ARS), NY/ADAGP, Paris.

Self-Portrait, by Pierre Auguste Renoir. c. 1875, oil on canvas, 39.1 x 31.7 cm. © Sterling and Francine Clark Art Institute, Williamstown, MA.

Portrait of Sisley, by Pierre Auguste Renoir. 1876, oil on canvas, 66.4 x 54.2. cm. © Bridgeman Art Library International Ltd., London/New York/Art Institute of Chicago, IL.

Self-Portrait, by Mary Cassatt. c. 1880, watercolor on paper, 33 x 24.4 cm. © Art Resource, NY/National Portrait Gallery, Smithsonian Institution, Washington, DC.

Camille Pissarro was older and more experienced than the other Impressionist artists. Because he was very kind and generous, he often spent time teaching and guiding his friends.

Self-Portrait, by Edgar Degas. c. 1862, oil on canvas, 92 x 69 cm. © Bridgeman Art Library International Ltd., London/New York/Museu Calouste Gulbenkian, Lisbon, Portugal.

Self-Portrait, by Paul Cezanne. 1877, oil on canvas, 55.5 x 46 cm. © Bridgeman Art Library International Ltd., London/New York/Neue Pinakothek, Munich, Germany.

Self-Portrait (Les Miserables), by Paul Gauguin. 1888, oil on canvas, 45 x 55 cm. © Bridgeman Art Library International Ltd., London/New York/Rijksmuseum Vincent van Gogh, Amsterdam, Netherlands.

Self Portrait with Straw Hat, by Vincent van Gogh. 1887, oil on canvas, 41 x 33 cm. © Bridgeman Art Library International Ltd., London/New York/Rijksmusem Vincent van Gogh, Amsterdam, Netherlands, photo by J.P. Zenobel.

Artists such as Claude Monet, Pierre Auguste Renoir, Alfred Sisley, Mary Cassatt, Edgar Degas, Paul Cézanne, Paul Gauguin, and Vincent van Gogh respected Camille Pissarro and were thankful for his advice.

Jallais Hill, Pontoise, by Camille Pissarro. 1867, oil on canvas, 87 x 114.9 cm.
© Metropolitan Museum of Art, Bequest of William Church Osborn, 1951. (51.30.2).

Many of Camille Pissarro's most famous works are pictures of the countryside around Paris. Camille loved nature more than anything. He often showed roads leading into beautiful country villages.

The Hermitage at Pontoise, by Camille Pissarro. c. 1867, oil on canvas, 59 5/8 x 79 in.
© Solomon R. Guggenheim Museum, New York, Thannhauser Collection, Gift, Justin K. Thannhauser, 1978 (78.2514.67), photo by David Heald.

Camille usually included people walking along the roads. Sometimes these neighborly people seem to invite you to enter the friendly paintings.

Pissarro's quick little brush strokes and bright colors bring his paintings alive with color and with a feeling of natural, flickering sunlight.

The Vegetable Garden with Trees in Blossom, by Camille Pissarro. 1877, oil on canvas, 65.5 x 81 cm.
© Bridgeman Art Library International Ltd., London/New York/Musée d'Orsay, Paris, France/Giraudon.

Landscape at Eragny, by Camille Pissarro. 1895, oil on canvas, 60 x 73.4 cm.
© Art Resource, NY/Musée d'Orsay, Paris, France, photograph by Erich Lessing.

Camille Pissarro and his Impressionist friends weren't interested in showing finished details in their paintings. They were more interested in giving an impression of a wonderful moment in time.

Camille Pissarro had always been interested in drawing and art. When he was growing up, his family owned and ran a store that supplied shipping companies with food and supplies for their long journeys. Camille's parents hoped he would help run the family business some day.

Camille had other ideas. He spent most of his time sketching the full-masted ships in the St. Thomas harbor. He also loved drawing the people of St. Thomas and the sailors who came from faraway lands.

Bananeros (Banana Trees), by Camille Pissarro. 1852-1854, watercolor and pencil on paper, 33.5 x 47.2 cm. © Banco Central de Venezuela.

When Camille was twenty-two years old, he left St. Thomas. He and an artist friend went to the South American country of Venezuela to perfect their drawing skills. Camille made lots of drawings and watercolors of small villages and tropical jungles there.

Excursion to Mont Avila, Venezuela, by Camille Pissarro. 1854, pen and india ink with brush over pencil, 26.9 x 37.7 cm. © Ashmolean Museum, Oxford.

When Camille returned after two years, his parents realized that their son wasn't the least bit interested in working at their store. They agreed to let Camille travel to Paris, France. There he could get the best art training and have a chance at making a living as an artist.

The Death of Francesca de Rimini and Paolo Malatesta, by Alexandre Cabanel. 1870, oil on canvas, 184 x 255 cm.
© Art Resource, NY/Musée d'Orsay, Paris, France, photograph by Erich Lessing.

Camille Pissarro arrived in Paris in 1855. He couldn't believe all the artists and paintings he saw. There were art galleries, painting exhibits, and art museums all over the place. Many of these works of art were skillfully done and showed lots of detail, like the painting shown above. But most of these paintings didn't interest him very much.

Although this was the style of the day, Camille thought these types of paintings looked too staged. Camille did like the work of one artist, though. His name was Camille Corot. Pissarro loved Corot's paintings of nature. He liked the way Corot gave a silvery glow to his scenes. Corot was known for helping young artists, and he often gave Camille Pissarro advice.

The Road to Sin-le-Noble, near Douai, by Jean-Baptiste Camille Corot. 1873, oil on canvas, 60 x 81 cm.
© Art Resource, NY/Réunion des Musées Nationaux, photo by H. Lewandowski.

Camille Pissarro wasn't too crazy about the idea of taking art classes. He preferred to learn on his own or from other artists. To make his father happy, though, he agreed to take some classes at one of the best art schools in Paris.

Camille also promised his father he would try to get his work into the most important art show in France, the Paris Salon. The Salon judges accepted only the types of paintings Camille really didn't care for. But since he had made a promise, Camille worked as hard as he could—and he did get a painting into the show!

Mr. and Mrs. Pissarro decided to move to Paris around this time. Camille's father arrived in Paris just in time to see the exhibit. Even though Camille's painting was hung way up high so hardly anyone could see it, Mr. Pissarro was thrilled and very proud of his son.

Mr. Pissarro wasn't happy for long, though. His son was lucky to get a painting in the Salon show, but he wasn't very lucky when it came to selling his work. Camille's parents worried a lot about how Camille would make a living.

Camille and his family at Eragny, c. 1885. © Musée Camille Pissarro, Pontoise.

They worried even more when Camille fell in love with the family housemaid. Her name was Julie Vellay. Julie and Camille ended up getting married and having lots of children.

Camille wasn't worried about his future. He always believed he could make a living as an artist. It was never easy for him, though. Every time things seemed to be going well, something would come up to ruin his plans.

When a war broke out in France in 1870, Camille took his family to London, England, where they would be safe. While Camille was away, enemy soldiers broke into his home in France. They used his house as a stable. They also destroyed more than a thousand of Camille Pissarro's drawings and paintings.

Sometimes the soldiers used Pissarro's paintings to wipe their muddy boots on, or burned them in the fireplace! When Camille returned home, he was shocked. But instead of giving up, he was determined to make his next paintings even better than the ones that had been destroyed.

Camille Pissarro always worked very hard. He painted from early morning till sunset almost every day. One of Camille's favorite things to do when he got home was teach his children to draw pictures and appreciate art.

Even with all his hard work, Camille's family was often nearly starving. Aside from a few art collectors, hardly anyone was interested in buying Pissarro's pictures.

Once, when Pissarro showed a smokestack in one of his paintings, people became angry. They couldn't believe an artist would paint anything as ugly as a smokestack. Camille knew, though, that everything he put in his painting was a part of the real world and could be beautiful in its own way.

The River Oise near Pontoise, by Camille Pissarro. 1873, oil on canvas, 45.3 x 55 cm.
© Sterling and Francine Clark Art Institute, Williamstown, MA.

La Loge, by Pierre Auguste Renoir. 1874, oil on canvas, 80 x 63 cm. © Bridgeman Art Library International Ltd., London/New York/Courtauld Gallery, London, UK.

Boulevard des Capucines, by Claude Monet. 1873, oil on canvas, 61 x 80 cm. © Bridgeman Art Library International Ltd., London/New York/Pushkin Museum, Moscow, Russia.

The Dancing Class, by Hilaire-Germain-Edgar Degas. 1871-1872, oil on wood, 19.7 x 27 cm. © Metropolitan Museum of Art, H.O. Havemeyer Collection, Bequest of Mrs. H.O. Havemeyer, 1929. (29.100.184).

The House of the Hanged Man, by Paul Cézanne. 1873, oil on canvas, 55 x 66 cm. © Bridgeman Art Library International Ltd., London/New York/Musée d'Orsay, Paris, France.

Camille Pissarro's artist friends were having trouble selling their paintings, too. They all decided to put on an exhibit so everyone could see their work and learn to appreciate it. Some of the paintings from that exhibit are shown above.

White Frost, by Camille Pissarro. 1873, oil on canvas, 65 x 93 cm. © Bridgeman Art Library International Ltd., London/New York/Musée d'Orsay, Paris, France/Giraudon.

Unfortunately, almost everyone who came to see the show made fun of the paintings. Some people were outraged that Renoir, Monet, Degas, Cézanne, and Pissarro would dare to paint just "impressions" of a scene. It was during this exhibit in 1874 that Camille Pissarro and his friends became known as the Impressionists.

Rabbit Warren at Pontoise, Snow, by Camille Pissarro. 1879, oil on canvas, 59.2 x 72.3 cm.
© The Art Institute of Chicago, Gift of Marshall Field, 1964.200.

The first Impressionist exhibit seemed like a big mistake. Even though Camille Pissarro was very disappointed, he continued to work harder than ever painting his beautiful scenes of villages, forests, and everyday people.

The Pork Butcher,
by Camille Pissarro.
1883, oil on canvas,
64.1 x 54.3 cm.
© Art Resource,
NY/Tate Gallery,
London, Great
Britain.

Camille believed that he and his friends
were doing exactly the right thing. He knew
that someday people would realize how
beautiful Impressionist art really was.

Camille Pissarro was right. It took many years of struggling, though, before the Impressionists' work became popular. When Camille was almost sixty years old, he began to sell lots of paintings. He finally started making enough money to live very well.

The Cote des Boeufs at L'Hermitage, Pontoise, by Camille Pissarro. 1877, oil on canvas, 114.9 x 87.6 cm.
© Bridgeman Art Library International Ltd., London/New York/National Gallery, London, UK.

Avenue de l'Opera, sun, winter morning, by Camille Pissarro. 1898, oil on canvas, 73 x 91.8 cm.
© Art Resource, NY/Réunion des Musées Nationaux, photo by Gerard Blot.

Later in his life, Camille Pissarro started having problems with one of his eyes. His doctor didn't want him outdoors in the wind and dust. Camille began to rent rooms in hotels. He would look down from his hotel window and paint beautiful street scenes from safe inside his room.

The Fair at Dieppe,
A Sunny Afternoon,
by Camille Pissarro.
1901, oil on canvas,
73 x 91. 8 cm.
© Philadelphia Museum
of Art, Bequest of
Lisa Norris Elkins.

The Boulevard Montmartre
at Night, by Camille
Pissarro. 1897, oil on
canvas, 53.3 x 64.8 cm.
© Bridgeman Art Library
International Ltd.,
London/New
York/National Gallery,
London, UK.

Camille Pissarro died in 1903 at the age of seventy-three. He spent most of his life creating wonderful drawings, prints, and paintings of simple, everyday scenes. Pissarro inspired many great artists of his time. He helped keep the Impressionist artists together as a group by settling their arguments, encouraging them, and showing them how important it was to never give up.

Works of art in this book can be seen at the following places:

The Art Institute of Chicago

Ashmolean Museum, Oxford

Courtauld Gallery, London

Dallas Museum of Art

Metropolitan Museum of Art, New York

Musée d'Orsay, Paris

Museu Calouste Gulbenkian, Lisbon

National Gallery, London

National Portrait Gallery, Smithsonian Institution, Washington, D.C.

Neue Pinakothek, Munich

Philadelphia Museum of Art

Pushkin Museum, Moscow

Réunion des Musées Nationaux, Paris

Rijksmuseum Vincent van Gogh, Amsterdam

Solomon R. Guggenheim Museum, New York

Sterling and Francine Clark Art Institute, Williamstown

Tate Gallery, London